SECRETS TO SUCCESS IN THE INSURANCE BUSINESS

ESSENTIAL SKILLS FOR LIFE INSURANCE AGENTS

DR. D. N. RAIZADAY

Contents

Preface

Writing *Secrets to Success in the Insurance Business: Essential Tips for Life Insurance Agents* has been an exciting new endeavor for me. With years of experience both in academia as a Professor of Zoology and as an advisor with Max Life Insurance, I've had the opportunity to understand the journey of a life insurance agent from a unique perspective. Transitioning into the insurance industry brought its own challenges and opportunities, but my approach to this field has always been fueled by a desire to empower others with knowledge and confidence.

Since joining Max Life in 2015, I've learned that a successful career in life insurance is built on a strong foundation of essential skills, resilience, and, above all, confidence. This book is a compilation of the principles, strategies, and personal insights that have been pivotal in my own achievements. From the initial days when I achieved the MDRT *(Million Dollar Round Table)* status to the years of sustained success, I've recognized that success in life insurance is as much about communication, empathy, and preparation as it is about policies and numbers.

Secrets to Success in the Insurance Business is written for both new and experienced agents who wish to build a lasting career in life insurance. The chapters within offer guidance on core areas such as effective communication, client engagement, handling objections, and time management. These skills, often overlooked, are what truly set apart successful agents. My goal with this book is to inspire confidence in every reader, equipping you not only with skills but with the mindset necessary to thrive.

I hope that the insights and practical advice in this book serve as valuable tools for you as you navigate and succeed in the rewarding career of life insurance.

Dr. Deepak Narain Raizaday

CHAPTER ONE

Introduction to Life Insurance Sales

Understanding Life Insurance

1. Life insurance offers financial protection by providing a payout to beneficiaries after the policyholder's death.
2. Policies like **term life insurance** provide temporary coverage, typically for 10-30 years, while **permanent life insurance** (whole or universal life) offers lifelong protection.
3. **Term insurance** is affordable and appeals to young families, while **whole life insurance** builds cash value that can be borrowed against.
4. Agents must understand the **underwriting process**, which evaluates health, age, and lifestyle to determine risk.
5. Addressing misconceptions about life insurance's affordability and necessity is crucial for convincing clients.
6. Clients need to view life insurance as a crucial component of their broader financial security plan, offering essential protection for loved ones and ensuring financial stability in adversity.

The Role of a Life Insurance Agent

1. Agents serve as **financial advisors**, helping clients choose policies that match their financial goals and needs.
2. Trust and rapport are essential; clients are more likely to buy from agents they feel comfortable with.
3. A key role of the agent is **educating clients** on the benefits of life insurance, including covering debts and protecting against financial loss.
4. Agents must continuously **update their knowledge** about new products, industry regulations, and client preferences.
5. Effective agents focus on building **long-term relationships** with clients, not just one-time sales.
6. Time management and organizational skills are crucial for balancing meetings, follow-ups, and administrative work.

Key Attributes of Successful Agents

1. **Empathy** helps agents understand their clients' emotional and financial concerns, building deeper trust.
2. **Resilience** is vital in handling rejection and persisting in a challenging industry where setbacks are common.
3. Agents with strong **communication skills** can convey complex information clearly and listen attentively to clients' needs.
4. Successful agents invest in **ongoing education** to stay up-to-date on insurance products and industry trends.
5. **Networking** with professionals such as financial planners or estate attorneys opens up referral opportunities and new business.

6. **Proactivity** in staying organized and self-motivated leads to increased sales and better career satisfaction.

• 3 •

CHAPTER TWO

Building Confidence

The Importance of Self-Confidence

1. Self-confidence is essential for building client trust and improving the overall sales experience.
2. Agents with strong confidence are more likely to convey the value of life insurance effectively, leading to more sales.
3. **Product knowledge** is the foundation of confidence; understanding policies inside and out reassures clients.
4. New agents can build confidence by practicing presentations and refining their sales approach through role-playing.
5. Confident agents are better equipped to handle objections and rejections without being discouraged.
6. A positive attitude and confidence lead to better client relationships and long-term career satisfaction.

Overcoming Fear of Rejection

1. Fear of rejection is common but manageable through preparation and a focus on relationship-building over sales outcomes.

2. Agents should view rejection as part of the sales process, learning from each experience to improve.
3. **Reframing rejection** as a learning opportunity helps agents stay motivated and improve with each client interaction.
4. Building **rapport and trust** with clients reduces the sting of rejection, as the focus shifts to long-term relationships.
5. Practicing pitches and handling objections in a **low-pressure setting** like role-playing can reduce anxiety.
6. Agents can draw strength from **support networks**—mentors, colleagues, or peers—to boost their resilience.

Techniques to Boost Confidence

1. **Visualization** helps agents mentally prepare for client meetings by imagining successful outcomes.
2. Role-playing with colleagues helps agents practice handling objections and refining their sales technique.
3. Setting small, achievable goals provides a **positive feedback loop** that builds confidence over time.
4. Continuous education—attending workshops and completing certifications—instills a sense of expertise and readiness.
5. **Networking** with supportive peers and mentors can help reinforce self-belief and provide valuable feedback.
6. Confidence grows from experience; the more interactions agents have with clients, the more naturally confident they become.

CHAPTER THREE

Mastering Communication Skills

Active Listening Techniques

1. **Active listening** involves giving clients your full attention, showing you value their input and concerns.
2. Maintaining eye contact, nodding, and providing verbal affirmations like "I understand" encourage clients to share more.
3. Summarizing and paraphrasing client concerns enhances mutual understanding, fosters clear communication, and establishes a foundation of trust.
4. Deferring judgment and avoiding interruptions create a safe space for clients to express their thoughts freely.
5. Active listening helps agents uncover deeper client needs that may not be immediately apparent, leading to more tailored solutions.
6. Mastering this essential skill significantly strengthens the agent-client relationship, fostering trust and understanding, while greatly increasing the likelihood of successfully closing sales and achieving client satisfaction.

Effective Questioning Strategies

1. **Open-ended questions** invite clients to express their thoughts in detail, offering deeper insight into their needs.
2. Probing questions help clients explore concerns they may not have initially considered, allowing agents to address specific needs.
3. **Reflective questions** encourage clients to rethink their views, leading to more meaningful discussions.
4. Closed-ended questions help clarify specific details, such as previous insurance coverage or financial goals.
5. Using the right mix of questions ensures agents gather all the necessary information to offer appropriate solutions.
6. Effective questioning builds rapport and shows clients that the agent genuinely cares about their needs.

Explaining Complex Concepts Simply

1. Use **analogies** and relatable examples to simplify complicated insurance concepts, making them easier to grasp.
2. Visual aids, like diagrams or charts, break down complex ideas into digestible parts for clients.
3. Tailor explanations to the client's level of understanding, avoiding technical jargon where unnecessary.
4. Encourage clients to ask questions, creating an interactive and open dialogue.
5. Repeat key points throughout the conversation to reinforce understanding and retention.

6. Simplifying complex ideas builds confidence in clients and makes them more comfortable making informed decisions.

CHAPTER FOUR

Understanding Your Product

Types of Life Insurance Policies

1. **Term life insurance** provides coverage for a specific time frame (e.g., 10-30 years) and is often more affordable than permanent insurance.
2. **Whole life insurance** offers lifelong coverage with the added benefit of cash value accumulation.
3. **Universal life insurance** allows flexibility in premium payments and death benefits, making it adaptable to changing financial circumstances.
4. **Variable life insurance** includes an investment component, where policyholders can invest in different portfolios, offering growth potential.
5. **Indexed universal life insurance** ties cash value growth to a stock market index, appealing to clients seeking moderate growth with lower risk.
6. Agents must thoroughly understand these different policy types to provide well-suited recommendations tailored specifically to each client's unique needs, financial goals, and long-term security objectives.

Key Features and Benefits

1. **Death benefit**: The primary feature of life insurance, ensuring financial protection for beneficiaries after the policyholder's death.
2. **Cash value accumulation**: Permanent policies like whole life allow clients to build savings that can be borrowed against or withdrawn.
3. **Premium structure**: Policies can offer level, increasing, or decreasing premiums, impacting affordability and long-term cost.
4. **Tax advantages**: Cash value grows tax-deferred, and death benefits are typically tax-free for beneficiaries.
5. **Flexibility**: Universal life and other policies provide options to adjust coverage and premium levels over time.
6. **Estate planning**: Whole and universal life insurance can help clients with wealth transfer and estate planning strategies.

How to Explain Complex Concepts Simply

1. **Understand the client's knowledge level** to tailor explanations appropriately and avoid overwhelming them with jargon.
2. Use **analogies and relatable examples** to help clients grasp unfamiliar concepts, such as comparing life insurance to a safety net.
3. **Visual aids** like charts and infographics can break down complex ideas into simpler, digestible components.
4. **Explain key points clearly** and reinforce them with examples that relate to the client's personal situation or goals.

5. **Encourage questions** throughout the discussion to ensure the client fully understands the product.
6. **Repetition and reinforcement** of essential concepts ensure retention and build confidence in the client's decision-making process. •

CHAPTER FIVE

Prospecting and Lead Generation

Identifying Your Target Market

1. Defining the target market—by age, family status, income, and occupation—allows for more focused sales efforts.
2. Understand the client's **psychographics**, including their values and motivations, to better tailor your pitch.
3. Analyzing existing clients provides insight into the demographics most likely to engage with your services.
4. **Market segmentation** helps create targeted marketing strategies for specific groups, like young families or retirees.
5. Continuously reassess your target market to stay aligned with changing industry trends and client needs.
6. A well-defined target market makes it easier to create personalized pitches and attract the right prospects.

Strategies for Finding Leads

1. Leverage personal and professional networks to generate leads, focusing on building relationships for

long-term success.

2. **Online marketing** strategies, such as SEO and content marketing, can attract clients searching for insurance solutions.
3. Cold calling, while challenging, can yield results when agents focus on education rather than pushing for sales.
4. Collaborating with other professionals, like financial advisors, allows for **cross-referrals**.
5. Attending industry events or seminars is a great way to network and find new clients.
6. Following up with potential leads through emails or calls ensures prospects remain engaged.

Leveraging Referrals

1. **Satisfied clients** are a key source of referrals; ensure they feel valued to encourage recommendations.
2. Referral programs incentivize clients to recommend your services to friends and family.
3. Ask clients directly for referrals after successfully closing a deal; they are often willing to help.
4. Maintaining strong relationships with clients increases the likelihood of gaining valuable referrals.
5. Collaborate with other professionals to exchange referrals, expanding your network.
6. Thank clients who refer others to show appreciation and encourage future recommendations.

CHAPTER SIX

Conducting Effective Meetings

Preparing for Client Meetings

1. **Research the client's background** to understand their financial situation and needs, enabling you to tailor your presentation.
2. Create a **structured agenda** that covers key discussion points, such as current policies, financial goals, and recommended solutions.
3. **Prepare visual aids** like brochures and charts to simplify the explanation of complex policies.
4. **Practice your pitch** to deliver information confidently, including non-verbal cues like body language.
5. **Role-play potential scenarios** to refine your handling of objections or difficult questions.
6. **Confirm meeting logistics** (time, place, or virtual setup) to ensure a smooth, professional interaction.

Structuring Your Presentation

1. Begin with an **engaging introduction** that captures the client's attention, such as a relevant story or statistic.

2. **Outline the main points** you'll cover, helping the client follow along and understand the flow of the conversation.
3. Break the presentation into **logical sections**, such as explaining types of coverage or addressing misconceptions.
4. **Use transitional phrases** to move smoothly between topics, keeping the client engaged.
5. Incorporate **visual aids and examples** to clarify complex information.
6. End with a **clear conclusion** that summarizes the key benefits and encourages the client to take action.

Closing Techniques

1. **Assumptive close**: Act as though the client has already decided and ask, "When would you like to begin coverage?"
2. **Summary close**: Recap the benefits and key features before asking for the client's decision.
3. **Urgency close**: Highlight the potential consequences of delay, such as rising premiums or changing health.
4. **Alternative close**: Present two options (e.g., term or whole life) to guide the client towards a decision.
5. **Referral close**: Ask for referrals from satisfied clients at the close of the sale, e.g., "Who else could benefit from this solution?"

CHAPTER SEVEN

Handling Objections

Common Objections in Life Insurance Sales

1. Clients may object due to **perceived high costs** or thinking they don't need insurance.
2. Addressing **misunderstandings** about affordability and necessity is crucial.
3. **Lack of trust** or uncertainty about the benefits can also raise objections.
4. Clients may feel they have **sufficient coverage** elsewhere and not see the value in more.
5. **Misconceptions about policy terms** (e.g., "It won't pay out") need to be clarified.
6. **Timing concerns** (e.g., "I'll do it later") should be reframed to highlight urgency.

Techniques for Addressing Objections

1. Use the **"feel-felt-found" technique** to validate concerns and provide a positive solution.
2. **Empathize** with clients' concerns and show you understand their perspective.
3. Provide **case studies or testimonials** to demonstrate the benefits experienced by others in similar situations.

4. Offer **alternative solutions**, like different coverage levels or term lengths, to address budget concerns.
5. **Clarify misconceptions** about policy payouts or exclusions with clear facts.
6. **Reassure the client** about the long-term benefits of securing insurance early.

Turning Objections into Opportunities

1. View objections as an **opportunity to engage** clients in deeper conversation.
2. Use objections to **showcase your expertise** by addressing concerns confidently.
3. Acknowledge and **validate client concerns** to build trust.
4. Share **success stories** of clients who overcame similar objections and benefited.
5. **Follow up** with additional information or resources that address their specific concerns.
6. Turn objections into a chance to **educate and clarify**, strengthening the relationship.

CHAPTER EIGHT

Follow-Up Strategies

The Importance of Follow-Up

1. **Regular follow-up** helps keep potential clients engaged and moves them closer to a decision.
2. Clients often need time to consider options, so follow-ups maintain interest and remind them of the benefits.
3. **Consistency in communication** builds trust, showing that you are invested in their financial well-being.
4. Following up with **existing clients** ensures their policies still meet their changing needs and strengthens relationships.
5. **Following through** on client queries or concerns demonstrates professionalism and reliability.
6. A solid follow-up strategy can significantly **increase conversion rates** and overall client satisfaction.

Effective Follow-Up Techniques

1. **Segment clients** into categories like hot, warm, and cold leads to prioritize your follow-ups.
2. Use **CRM tools** to track interactions and schedule reminders for timely follow-ups.

3. **Personalize follow-up messages** based on previous conversations or specific client needs.
4. **Leverage automated emails** for consistent communication with prospects.
5. Incorporate **multiple follow-up methods** like phone calls, emails, or even social media messages.
6. Establish a **structured follow-up schedule** to ensure regular contact without overwhelming the client.

Maintaining Client Relationships

1. **Regular communication** keeps clients engaged, even after a sale, and demonstrates long-term commitment.
2. Sending **personalized updates** about policy changes or industry news fosters ongoing trust.
3. **Offer policy reviews** to ensure the client's coverage aligns with their evolving financial needs.
4. Celebrate **client milestones** (e.g., birthdays, anniversaries) with personalized messages.
5. **Promptly address concerns** or questions to reinforce reliability and client satisfaction.
6. Maintain **transparency and honesty** to foster trust and encourage long-term loyalty.

CHAPTER NINE

Time Management for Agents

Prioritizing Your Sales Activities

1. Focus on **high-impact activities** that directly contribute to sales, such as client meetings and follow-ups.
2. Use tools like the **Eisenhower Matrix** to categorize tasks by urgency and importance.
3. **Set clear goals** (daily, weekly, monthly) to stay focused on your priorities.
4. **Avoid time-wasters**, like excessive administrative work, by delegating where possible.
5. **Dedicate time** for client acquisition, policy reviews, and networking each week.
6. Regularly **review and adjust** your schedule to improve efficiency.

Tools and Techniques for Time Management

1. Use **digital calendars** to schedule appointments and block time for specific tasks like prospecting or follow-ups.

2. Implement **time-blocking** to stay focused on one task at a time, minimizing distractions.
3. **CRM systems** help keep track of client interactions and set reminders for follow-ups.
4. The **Pomodoro Technique** can improve focus by working in short, timed bursts with breaks.
5. **Automate routine tasks**, such as sending emails or follow-up reminders, to free up time for higher-value activities.
6. Set aside time for **reflection and adjustment** to refine your time management practices over time.

Setting and Achieving Sales Goals

1. Set **SMART goals** (Specific, Measurable, Achievable, Relevant, Time-bound) to guide your sales strategy.
2. Break long-term goals into **manageable steps** to stay motivated and focused.
3. **Track progress regularly** to identify areas for improvement and celebrate small wins.
4. Adjust your goals based on **market conditions** or personal performance.
5. **Hold yourself accountable** by reviewing your goals at the end of each week or month.
6. **Reward yourself** for hitting milestones to maintain motivation and momentum.

CHAPTER TEN

Continuing Education and Development

The Importance of Ongoing Training

1. **Ongoing education** helps agents stay updated on new products, regulations, and sales techniques.
2. **Deepening product knowledge** boosts confidence and improves client interactions.
3. Continuous training sharpens skills in **prospecting, communication, and closing sales**.
4. **Industry trends** are constantly evolving, and ongoing learning keeps you competitive.
5. Training helps agents **navigate complex scenarios**, improving their adaptability and problem-solving skills.
6. Investing in education shows clients that you are committed to offering the best service possible.

Resources for Professional Growth

1. **Industry publications and newsletters** provide insights into market trends and regulatory changes.
2. **Webinars, seminars, and workshops** offer opportunities for learning new strategies and

networking.

3. **Mentorship programs** provide guidance from experienced agents and help build confidence.
4. **Certifications** in specialized areas like advanced underwriting or estate planning can boost credibility.
5. **Online courses** allow flexibility and provide a broad range of topics to suit your learning needs.
6. **Peer groups** offer opportunities to share experiences, learn best practices, and gain new perspectives.

Staying Updated on Industry Changes

1. **Subscribe to industry news** to stay informed about evolving market conditions and new regulations.
2. Attend **conferences and webinars** to hear from industry experts and gain new perspectives.
3. **Join professional associations** to network with peers and access educational resources.
4. **Engage in online forums** to exchange ideas and stay connected with other professionals.
5. Regularly review updates from **regulatory bodies** to ensure compliance and remain competitive.
6. **Seek feedback** from clients and peers to identify emerging trends or areas for improvement.

CHAPTER ELEVEN

Building a Personal Brand

Defining Your Unique Selling Proposition

1. Identify your **unique strengths** and what differentiates you from other agents.
2. Focus on the specific **value you offer clients**, such as personalized service or specialized knowledge.
3. **Tailor your message** to the needs and preferences of your target market.
4. Use **client testimonials and success stories** to highlight your expertise.
5. Develop a **clear and consistent brand message** that reflects your values and approach.
6. Continuously refine your USP based on **client feedback and evolving market demands**.

Utilizing Social Media for Branding

1. Create a **professional profile** on platforms like LinkedIn, showcasing your expertise and services.
2. Share **valuable content** such as tips, articles, or case studies to position yourself as a thought leader.

3. **Engage with your audience** by responding to comments, answering questions, and participating in discussions.
4. Use **visuals and infographics** to make your content more engaging and shareable.
5. **Promote testimonials** and client success stories to build credibility.
6. **Regularly post updates** on industry news and personal insights to maintain visibility and relevance.

Networking for Success

1. **Attend industry events** like conferences or seminars to meet professionals and potential clients.
2. **Join professional associations** to expand your network and gain access to industry resources.
3. **Leverage social media** to connect with peers, share knowledge, and build a referral network.
4. **Participate in community activities** to meet potential clients and establish local credibility.
5. Seek **mentorship from experienced agents** to gain insights and expand your professional circle.
6. **Follow up with contacts** regularly to nurture relationships and create opportunities for collaboration.

CHAPTER TWELVE

Conclusion and Next Steps

Recap of Essential Skills

1. **Mastering communication** is essential for building trust and explaining complex insurance products clearly.
2. Building **long-term relationships** is key to generating referrals and repeat business.
3. **Handling objections** effectively strengthens your client-agent relationship and improves sales outcomes.
4. **Consistent follow-ups** with clients ensure ongoing engagement and satisfaction.
5. **Time management** helps prioritize high-impact activities and improves productivity.
6. **Ongoing education** is crucial to staying competitive and offering top-notch client service.

Setting Future Goals

1. Establish **SMART goals** for career growth and track progress regularly.
2. Break larger goals into **small, achievable steps** to maintain motivation.

3. **Adjust goals** as needed based on changing market conditions or personal performance.
4. **Celebrate milestones** to reinforce success and keep moving forward.
5. Build a plan for **continuous improvement** by seeking feedback and staying adaptable.
6. **Focus on long-term growth**, including expanding your client base and deepening industry expertise.

Encouragement for Lifelong Learning

1. Lifelong learning is essential for **staying relevant** and maintaining success in a rapidly evolving industry.
2. **Stay curious** and seek new knowledge, whether through formal training or self-study.
3. **Embrace change** and use challenges as opportunities to grow and improve your skills.
4. Regularly assess your strengths and areas for improvement, and **pursue further education** in those areas.
5. Surround yourself with **supportive peers and mentors** who encourage your growth.
6. Stay **open to new ideas** and continuously improve, ensuring long-term success in your career.